Usborne

my very first
Dinosaurs
book

Illustrated by Lee Cosgrove
Written by Alex Frith
Designed by Alice Reese
Dinosaur expert: Dr. Darren Naish

In the time of the dinosaurs

Long, long ago, before there were any people, planet Earth was home to creatures known as dinosaurs.

'Dinosaur' means 'terrible lizard'.
Some dinosaurs were big and frightening,
but others were surprisingly small.

Apatosaurus

Camarasaurus

Stokesosaurus

Allosaurus

Gargoyleosaurus

Some dinosaurs had scaly skin.
Others, like these, had feathers.

Othnielosaurus

Ornitholestes

Big and small

Dinosaurs were the largest animals that have ever walked on land. Nobody knows which type was the very biggest, because people keep finding bigger bones.

Some dinosaurs were rather small. The smallest we know of were around the size of a duck.

Human being

Microraptor

Minmi

Citipati

Protoceratops

Microceratus

Ankylosaurus

Compsognathus

This tail alone was the same length as a python.

These legs were twice the height of an adult human.

These horns were as long as a human arm.

Triceratops

Tyrannosaurus rex

This dinosaur's head was almost as big as a human being.

This dinosaur lived in water.

Spinosaurus

This massive dinosaur was heavier than twenty elephants put together.

Its neck was at least three times longer than a giraffe's neck.

Diplodocus

Stegosaurus

Where did dinosaurs come from?

Dinosaurs weren't the first animals that lived on the Earth. Before them, came crawling animals – and even before them, there were swimming animals in the sea.

Jellyfish

Trilobites

The very first animals swam or floated under water. They had no arms or legs.

Tiktaalik

Fish with flippers were the first creatures to crawl out of the water.

Eryops

Dimetrodon

Some of the first animals that lived on land were scaly creatures a little like dinosaurs. Their legs stuck out on either side, and they crawled with their bellies close to the ground.

The very first dinosaurs appeared – along with lots of other animals – many, many years later. These dinosaurs walked on two legs, that stuck straight down under their bodies.

Mussaurus

Riojasaurus

Staurikosaurus

Herrerasaurus

Exaeretodon
(not a dinosaur)

Eoraptor

Ischigualastia
(not a dinosaur)

Inside a dinosaur

No one really knows what any dinosaur looked like on the outside. But we know a lot about their bones, and some other inside parts, too.

The bones in a skeleton reveal a lot about what shape a dinosaur was. The blue outline shows the shape of an Argentinosaurus – an enormous plant-eating dinosaur.

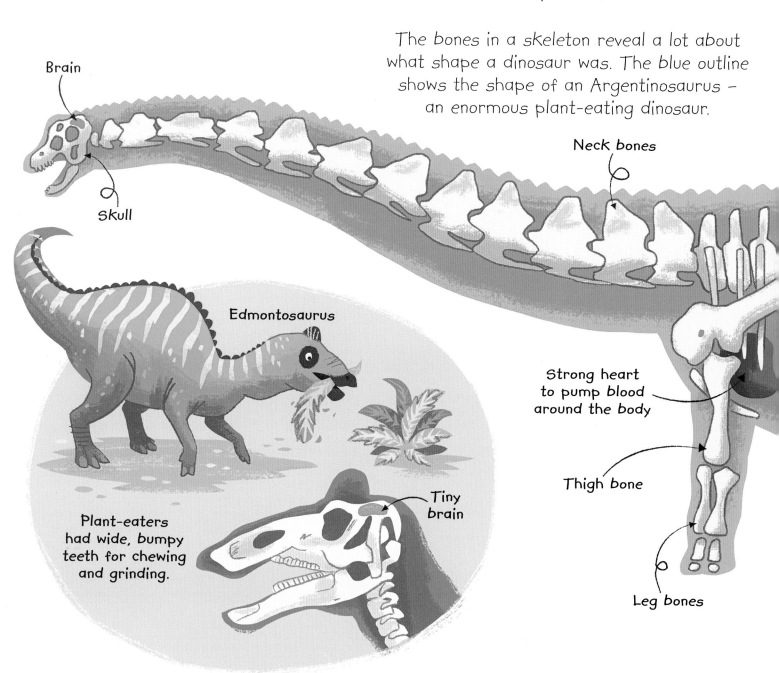

Brain

Skull

Neck bones

Edmontosaurus

Strong heart to pump blood around the body

Thigh bone

Plant-eaters had wide, bumpy teeth for chewing and grinding.

Tiny brain

Leg bones

Plant-eating dinosaurs chewed their food very thoroughly.

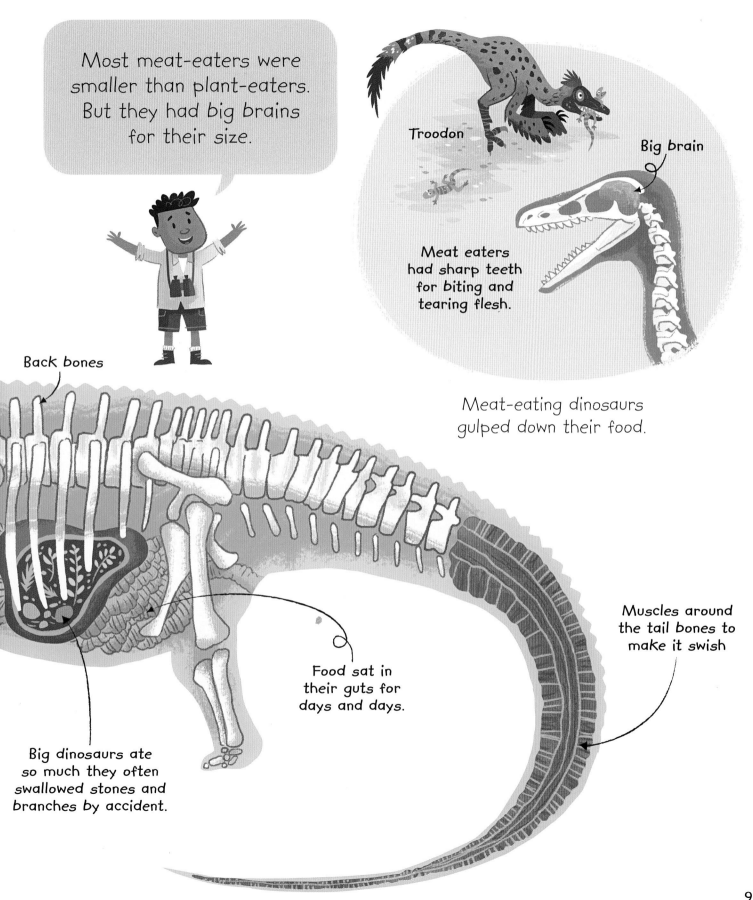

Most meat-eaters were smaller than plant-eaters. But they had big brains for their size.

Troodon

Big brain

Meat eaters had sharp teeth for biting and tearing flesh.

Meat-eating dinosaurs gulped down their food.

Back bones

Big dinosaurs ate so much they often swallowed stones and branches by accident.

Food sat in their guts for days and days.

Muscles around the tail bones to make it swish

Growing up

All dinosaurs, big and small, hatched from eggs.
Even the largest dinosaurs laid eggs that were
no bigger than a football.

A mother Citipati has just
laid a clutch of eggs.

The father sits on the nest
to keep the eggs warm.

Inside each egg, a tiny
baby Citipati grows.

After a few weeks, the
eggs are ready to hatch.

The babies peck their
way out from inside.

The parents bring food
for the children.

Some dinosaurs grew up in small groups called packs, or in enormous herds. Others lived on their own.

A lone hunter

Maiasaurus graze together in large herds.

Ornithomimus roam in a pack.

These dinosaurs are a year old. They're nearly adult-sized already.

Some dinosaurs leave their eggs to hatch on their own.

These Maiasaurus babies have just hatched.

Dinosaur battles

Dinosaurs got into fights all the time – over food, living space or to prove how tough they were.

This hungry Velociraptor wants to eat the Protoceratops...

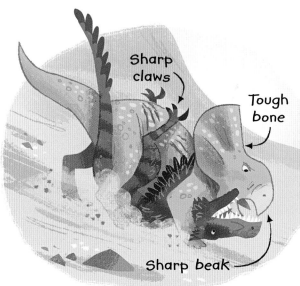

...but the Protoceratops isn't going to make it easy for her!

These two are having a head-butting competition.

They are probably fighting to be in charge of their herd.

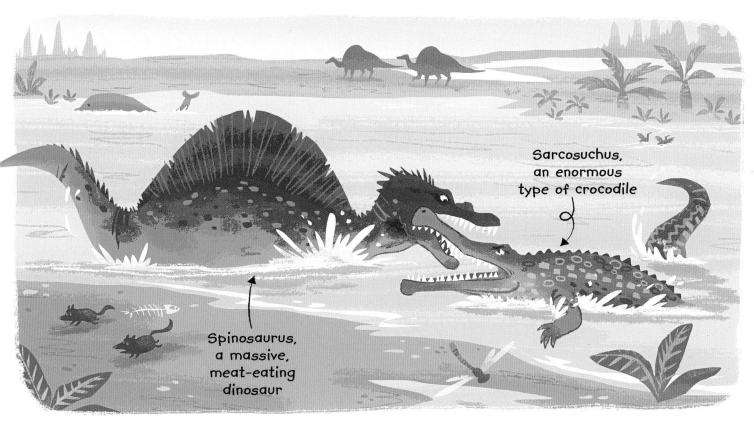

Sarcosuchus, an enormous type of crocodile

Spinosaurus, a massive, meat-eating dinosaur

These reptiles are fighting over hunting grounds around a river.

Allosaurus

Stegosaurus

This Stegosaurus is protecting her baby from a hungry Allosaurus.

Tail covered in sharp spikes

With a whip of her tail, she fends off the meat-eater's attack.

Up in the air

While dinosaurs roamed on land, flying creatures
known as pterosaurs soared through the sky.

Here are some pterosaurs
that lived by the sea.

Pterodactylus

Gnathosaurus

Scaphognathus

Rhamphorhynchus

Aerodactylus

Anurognathus

From end to end, these wings spread the length of a bus.

Bright crest

Hatzegopteryx

Pterosaurs were the biggest flying creatures that have ever existed.

Archaeopteryx

Confuciusornis

Quetzalcoatlus

Standing up, a Quetzalcoatlus was as tall as a giraffe.

Pterosaurs weren't the only animals with wings. Some dinosaurs had wings they used for gliding or flying.

15

Under the sea

In the time of the dinosaurs, massive creatures with big teeth prowled the oceans.

Plesiosaurus

Ichthyosaurus

Excalibosaurus

Macroplata

Rhomaleosaurus

Stenopterygius

Callipterus

Shark

Coelacanth

Mosasaurus

Giant squid

Platecarpus

Around the time most dinosaurs died out, the sea was home to all sorts of fierce creatures with sharp teeth or long tentacles.

Tylosaurus

Elasmosaurus

Ammonites

Dinosaurs in love

Many dinosaurs had striking features that made them look more attractive to each other – to help them find mates to have babies with.

Styracosaurus

Kosmoceratops

These animals had horns around their heads.
Some horns were long and pointed, others were curly.

Parasaurolophus

Tsintaosaurus

Corythosaurus

These dinosaurs had crests sticking out of their heads. Some could blow air through their crests, making a loud noise to say, "Look at me!"

Concavenators had big humps on their backs. Some could grow long feathers on their arms, too, for extra showing off.

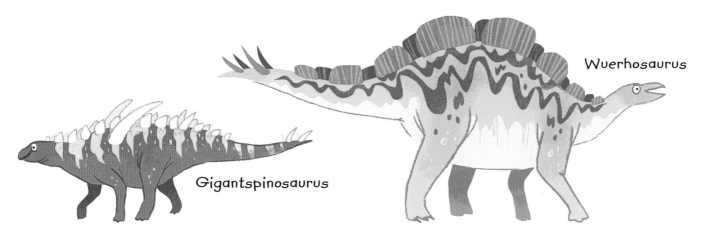

Gigantspinosaurus

Wuerhosaurus

Some dinosaurs displayed bony plates along their backs.

My, what big spines you have!

Agustinia had two rows of spines along its neck and back, as well as sharp spikes on the end of its tail.

Dinosaur hot, dinosaur cold

Dinosaurs lived all over the Earth, from scorching deserts to thick jungles to sprawling forests.

Protoceratops

Gallimimus

Velociraptor

Pinacosaurus

Linhenykus

Citipati

These dinosaurs all lived in the dry and dusty deserts of what is now central China.

Titanosaur

Vegavis

Atlascopcosaurus

Antarctopelta

Koolasuchus
(not a dinosaur)

Leaellynasaura

Trinisaura

These animals all lived in Antarctica. In those days, it wasn't covered in snow and ice. Instead, it was a dark and misty forest.

King of the dinosaurs

One of the biggest and scariest dinosaurs was Tyrannosaurus rex – possibly the largest meat-eater that has ever walked on two legs.

Each tooth was bigger than a person's foot.

The name 'Tyrannosaurus rex' means 'Tyrant lizard King'.

No one knows why it had such small arms.

Sometimes, Tyrannosaurus hunted animals for food.

Tyrannosaurus was also a scavenger, who ate animals that had already died.

Tyrannosaurus rex wasn't the only tyrannosaur. There were other, smaller ones, and some were covered in fluffy feathers, too.

Qianzhousaurus
(Nicknamed 'Pinocchio rex' because of its long snout)

Zhuchengtyrannus
(King of Zhucheng)

Daspletosaurus
(Frightful dinosaur)

Tarbosaurus
(Alarming dinosaur)

Teratophoneus
(Murderous monster)

Nanuqsaurus
(Polar bear dinosaur)

Albertosaurus
(Dinosaur from Alberta)

What happened to the dinosaurs?

Many millions of years ago, a huge disaster killed off all kinds of animals, including dinosaurs. Scientists are still trying to learn exactly how it happened.

It all began when an enormous rock from space came crashing into planet Earth...

...the rock made a hole in a place called Yucatan, on the east coast of Mexico.

Alamosaurus

Tyrannosaurus

Edmontosaurus

Triceratops

Tylosaurus

The crashing rock set off many
earthquakes and tsunamis.

Huge clouds of dust
filled the sky.

The dust spread out
and covered the Earth.

It grew cold and dark,
and many plants died out...

...so all the plant-eating
dinosaurs died out, too.

And, in time, so did
the meat-eaters.

But a few small animals survived. These included furry
mammals, and feathered dinosaurs – now called birds.

Bones and fossils

Dinosaur hunters are called paleontologists.
They dig into the ground to find the remains
of long-dead dinosaurs.

Millions of years ago...

A dinosaur dies and its
body is covered in mud.

Its body rots away,
leaving only a *skeleton*.

Hundreds of years later, it's
buried under layers of rocks.

When it rains, water
trickles into the bones.

Chemicals in the water
react with the bones...

...and slowly turn
them into fossils.

Millions of years later...

Rain and wind wear away
the rocks and the fossils.

A few fossils end up near
the surface of the soil...

...where a fossil hunter
can find them.

Paleontologists dig up
the fossils very carefully.

Then they scrape
all the dirt off.

Often, many fossil
bones are missing.

**Paleontologists make
new bones to fill in
any missing pieces.**

Paleontologists have to work out how all the bones fit together.

Dinosaurs today

You can *see* dinosaurs and other prehistoric animals in museums all over the world.

29

The changing world of dinosaurs

Dinosaurs didn't all live at the same time. Over the years, they appeared in many different shapes and sizes, too.

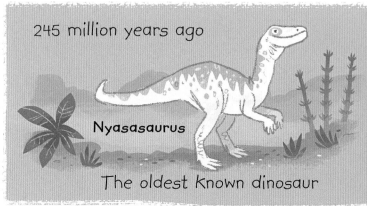

245 million years ago

Nyasasaurus

The oldest Known dinosaur

110 million years ago

Aquilops

The first dinosaurs with horns

150 million years ago

Archaeopteryx

The oldest Known birds

90 million years ago

Argentinosaurus

The biggest Known dinosaurs

Timeline of animals

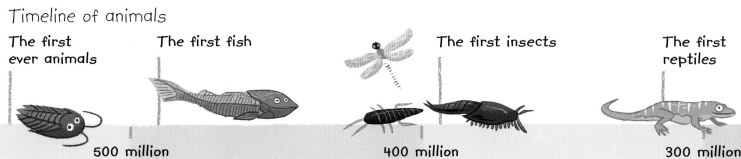

The first ever animals

The first fish

The first insects

The first reptiles

500 million years ago

400 million years ago

300 million years ago

230 million years ago

Plateosaurus

The first long-necked dinosaurs

220 million years ago

Eudimorphodon

The first pterosaurs

Coelophysis

200 million years ago

The first known pack dinosaurs

210 million years ago

Shastasaurus

The biggest ever undersea reptiles

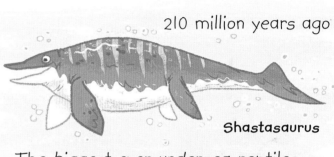

66 million years ago

Ornithomimus

The fastest known dinosaurs

64 million years ago

The only surviving dinosaurs: birds

The first dinosaurs

A great disaster kills off many animals

The first people

200 million years ago

100 million years ago

Now

Index

Series Editor: Ruth Brocklehurst   Series Designer: Nicola Butler